IN RECITAL®
for the Advancing Pianist
Jazz & Blues

ABOUT THE SERIES

In Recital® for the Advancing Pianist continues the ever-popular six-book *In Recital®* series by showcasing jazz and blues works for the pianist at the early advanced level. In this series, you will find expertly arranged well-known and much loved jazz and blues gems, as well as two original jazz compositions by Edwin McLean and Kevin Olson. Students will experience walking bass figures, swing, bebop, boogie-woogie, traditional blues, and stride bass; as well as jazz ballads and Latin jazz. The works in this series are true crowd pleasers that will capture the attention of audiences and show pianists in their best possible light. The wide variety of jazz and blues pieces for the Advancing Pianist will certainly fill many hours at the piano with delight. Enjoy the series!

Production: Frank J. Hackinson
Production Coordinators: Joyce Loke and Satish Bhakta
Cover Design: Terpstra Design, San Francisco, CA
Cover Art Concept: Helen Marlais
Cover Illustration: Keith Criss
Engraving: Tempo Music Press, Inc.
Printer: Tempo Music Press, Inc.

ISBN-13: 978-1-56939-795-4

TABLE OF CONTENTS

Railroad Blues

Music by C. Luckeyth Roberts Lyrics by Haven Gillespie and Howard Washington arr. Edwin McLean

Perdido

Music and Lyrics by Ervin Drake, Harry Lenk, and Juan Tizol — arr. Kevin Olson

NIGHT TRAIN

Music by Oscar Washington and Lewis Simpkins   Lyrics by Jimmy Forrest   arr. Edwin McLean

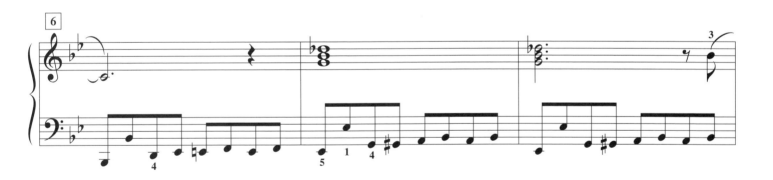

This Masquerade

Music and Lyrics by Leon Russell   arr. Kevin Olson

14

Freely; with rubato (♩ = 96)

Until This Moment

Edwin McLean

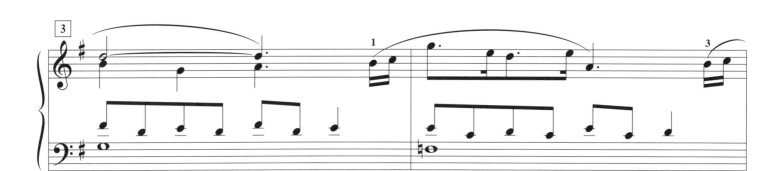

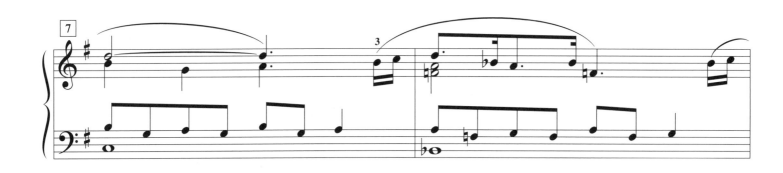

Beale Street Blues

Music and Lyrics by W.C. Handy   arr. Edwin McLean

FJH2087

My Foolish Heart

Music by Victor Young   Lyrics by Ned Washington   arr. Kevin Olson

24

HOUSE OF THE RISING SUN

Traditional   arr. Edwin McLean

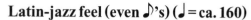

(with pedal)

Off-Balance Blues

Kevin Olson

Slow to moderate swing feel

The Saint Louis Blues

Music and Lyrics by W.C. Handy   arr. Kevin Olson

Fast Boogie feel (♩ = ca. 144) (♫ = ♩³♪)

36

Unforgettable

Music and Lyrics by Irving Gordon

Moderately slow; expressively (♩ = ca. 80)

40

FJH2087

Railroad Blues
Music: C. Luckeyth Roberts
Lyrics: Haven Gillespie and Howard Washington

My lovin' sweetie's gone,
My lovin' sweetie's gone away,
Yes, he's gone and run away,
Got the blues, got the blues,
Been a cryin' all the whole day through,
All I wanted was mah kissin';
But mah baby is a-missin' once again on a
    choo-choo train.
Engine whistles blowin',
Ding-dong, now he's goin':

Chorus:
I've got the feelin' bad,
I've got the feelin' bad.
I've got the feelin' called the railroad blues,
He didn't tell me why,
He didn't say goodbye,
Got everything I had except my shoes;
He left me flat just where I am an' blew,
That bird has flew.
Now all I do is think,
Can't even sleep a wink,
A-thinkin' of the things he has done for me.
An' every night it's cold, or else I'm getting old.
An' all he left me was a memory,
Oh! He was mine till the train pulled in with the blues,
Them railroad blues.

I wouldn't feel so bad,
But he was all I ever had,
He was all I ever had;
Lawd I'm broke, yes I'm broke,
But I'll hoof it till I run him down,
Tho my shoes may go to uppers
And my uppers go to nothin',
I'll be there, yes, I'll be there.
Engine whistles blowin',
Ding-dong, now he's goin':

Chorus

Perdido
Music and Lyrics: Ervine Drake, Harry Lenk,
and Juan Tizol

Perdido, I look for my heart, it's Perdido;
I lost it way down in Torrido
While chancing a dance fiesta.
Bolero, she glanced as she danced a bolero;
I said, taking off my sombrero, "Lets meet for a
    sweet siesta."

High was the sun when we first came close;
Low was the moon when we said "Adios!"

Perdido, since then my heart been Perdido;
I know I must go to Torrido, that yearning to
    lose Perdido.

Night Train
Music: Oscar Washington and Lewis Simpkins
Lyrics: Jimmy Forrest

Night train, that took my baby so far away.
Night train, that took my baby so far away.
Tell her I love her more and more ev'ry day.

My mother said I'd lose her if I ever did abuse her,
Should have listened.
My mother said I'd lose her if I ever did abuse her,
Should have listened.
Now I have learned my lesson, my sweet baby was
    a blessing,
Should have listened.

Night train, your whistle tore my poor heart in two.
Night train, your whistle tore my poor heart in two.
She's gone and I don't know what I'm gonna do.

This Masquerade
Music and Lyrics: Leon Russell

Are we really happy with this lonely game we play,
Looking for the right words to say?
Searching but not finding understanding anyway,
We're lost in this masquerade

Both afraid to say we're just too far away
From being close together from the start.
We tried to talk it over,
But the words got in the way;
We're lost inside this lonely game we play.

Thoughts of leaving disappear each time I see your eyes.
And no matter how hard I try
To understand the reason
Why we carry on this way,
We're lost in this masquerade.

Beale Street Blues
Music and Lyrics: W. C. Handy

I've seen the lights of gay Broadway,
Old Market Steet down by the Frisco Bay,
I've strolled the Prado, I've gambled on the Bourse,
The seven wonders of the world I've seen
And many are the places I have been.
Take my advice, folks, and see Beale Street first.

You'll see pretty Browns in beautiful gowns,
You'll see tailor-mades and hand-me-downs,
You'll meet honest men, and pick-pockets skilled,
You'll find that bus'ness never closes till somebody
    gets killed.

You'll see Hog-Nose rest'rants and Chitlin' Cafés,
You'll see Jugs that tell if bygone days,
And places, once places, now just a sham,
You'll see Golden Balls enough to pave the New
    Jerusalem.

If Beale Street could talk, If Beale Street could talk,
Married men would have to take their beds and walk,
Except one or two, who never drink booze,
And the blind man on the corner who sings the
    Beale Street Blues.

I'd rather be there than any place I know,
I'd rather be there than any place I know,
It's goin' to take the Sargent for to make me go,
Goin' to the river, maybe bye and bye,
Goin' to the river, and there's a reason why,
Because the river's wet, and Beale Street's done gone dry.

My Foolish Heart
Music: Victor Young
Lyrics: Ned Washington

The night is like a lovely tune, beware my foolish heart!
How white the ever constant moon;
Take care, my foolish heart!
There's a line between love and fascination
That's hard to see on an evening such as this,
For they give the very same sensation,
When you're lost in the passion of a kiss.
His lips are much too close to mine, beware my
    foolish heart,
But should our eager lips combine, then let the fire start.
For this time it isn't fascination, or a dream that
    will fade and fall apart,
It's love this time, it's love, my foolish heart!

House of the Rising Sun
Traditional

There is a house in New Orleans
They call the rising sun.
It's been the ruin of many a poor boy,
And God, I know I'm one.

My mother was a tailor,
She sewed my new blue jeans;
My father was a gambling man
Down in New Orleans.

Now the only thing a gambler needs
Is a suitcase and trunk,
And the only time he'll be satisfied
Is when he's on a drunk.

Oh mother, tell your children
Not to do what I have done;
Spend your lives in sin and misery
In the house of the rising sun.

The Saint Louis Blues
Music and Lyrics: W. C. Handy

I hate to see the evening sun go down,
Hate to see the evening sun go down,
'Cause my baby he done left this town.
Feelin' tomorrow, like I feel today,
Feel tomorrow, like I feel today,
I'll pack my trunk make my getaway.
St. Louis woman with her diamond rings,
Pulls that man 'round by her apron strings.
'Twasn't for powder and for store-bought hair,
The man I love would not gone nowhere.

Chorus:
Got the St. Louis blues, just as blue as I can be,
Than man got a heart like a rock cast in the sea,
Or else he wouldn't gone so far from me.
I love that man like a schoolboy loves his pie,
Like a Kentucky Colonel loves his mint and rye,
I'll love my baby till the day I die.

Doggone it!

Been to the Gypsy to get my fortune told
To the Gypsy done got my fortune told
Cause I'm is wild 'bout my Jelly Roll.
Gypsy done told me "don't you wear no black,"
Yes she done told me "don't you wear no black,"
Go to St. Louis and win him back.
Help me to Cairo,zs make St. Louis by myself,
Get to Cairo find my old friend Jeff.
Going to pin myself close to his side,
If I flag his train I sure can ride.

Chorus

You ought to see that stove pipe brown of mine
Like he owns the Diamond Joseph line,
He's make a cross-eyed woman go stone blind.
Blacker than midnight teeth like flags of truce,
Blackest man in the whole Saint Louis,
Blacker the berry, sweeter the juice.
About a crap game he knows a powerful lot
But when worktime comes, he's on the dot.
Going to ask him for a cold ten-spot,
What it takes to get it he's certainly got.

Chorus

Unforgettable
Music and Lyrics: Irving Gordon

Unforgettable, that's what you are.
Unforgettable, though near or far.
Like a song of love that clings to me,
How the thought of you does things to me;
Never before has someone been more

Unforgettable, in every way,
And forevermore, that's how you'll stay.
That's why, darling, it's incredible
That someone so unforgettable
Thinks that I am unforgettable too.

ABOUT THE ARRANGERS / COMPOSERS

Edwin McLean

Edwin McLean is a composer living in Chapel Hill, North Carolina. He is a graduate of the Yale School of Music, where he studied with Krzysztof Penderecki and Jacob Druckman. He also holds a master's degree in music theory and a bachelor's degree in piano performance from the University of Colorado.

Mr. McLean has been the recipient of several grants and awards: The MacDowell Colony, the John Work Award, the Woods Chandler Prize (Yale), Meet the Composer, Florida Arts Council, and many others. He has also won the Aliénor Composition Competition for his work *Sonata for Harpsichord*, published by The FJH Music Company Inc. and recorded by Elaine Funaro (*Into the Millennium*, Gasparo GSCD-331). His complete works for harpsichord are available on the Miami Bach Society recording, Edwin McLean: *Sonatas for 1, 2, and 3 Harpsichords*.

Since 1979, Edwin McLean has arranged the music of some of today's best-known recording artists. Currently, he is senior editor for The FJH Music Company Inc.

Kevin Olson

Kevin Olson is an active pianist, composer, and faculty member at Elmhurst College near Chicago, Illinois, where he teaches classical and jazz piano, music theory, and electronic music. He holds a Doctor of Education degree from National-Louis University, and bachelor's and master's degrees in music composition and theory from Brigham Young University. Before teaching at Elmhurst College, he held a visiting professor position at Humboldt State University in California.

A native of Utah, Kevin began composing at the age of five. When he was twelve, his composition *An American Trainride* received the Overall First Prize at the 1983 National PTA Convention in Albuquerque, New Mexico. Since then, he has been a composer-in-residence at the National Conference on Piano Pedagogy and has written music for the American Piano Quartet, Chicago a cappella, the Rich Matteson Jazz Festival, and several piano teachers associations around the country.

Kevin maintains a large piano studio, teaching students of a variety of ages and abilities. Many of the needs of his own piano students have inspired a diverse collection of books and solos published by The FJH Music Company Inc., which he joined as a writer in 1994.